Miguel Mennig

GW00602729

Shopping online

First published in the United Kingdom in 2001 by Hachette UK
ISBN 1 84202 082 X

Designed by M2M / Typeset in Sabon MT / Printed and bound in Germany

English translation by Prose Unlimited

Concept and editorial direction: Ghéorghiï Vladimirovitch Grigorieff

Additional editorial assistance: Simon Woolf, Derek Atkins

A CIP catalogue for this book is available from the British Library.

© Translation Hachette UK 2001

© Marabout 2001

Hachette UK

Cassell & Co

The Orion Publishing Group

Wellington House

125 Strand

London

WC2R 0BB

Table of Contents

Introduction

All the current surveys show that online shopping is set to grow significantly in the coming years. But is this fast-growing trend simply the result of new commercial strategies designed to trap the consumer? If this is so, then this little manual will help you to be on your guard against the evils of excessive commercialism. If, on the other hand, the Internet is fast becoming an integral element of international commerce – as appears to be the case – then it's precisely because there are real advantages to shopping this way.

The Internet really has brought us stress-free retail therapy. Your computer screen will, with a click of the mouse, enable you to go to the biggest supermarket in the country – or, indeed, the world – and you can switch from browsing CDs at a record store in New York to ordering a case of wine from a small vineyard in southern France. There is no longer any need to rush when it's nearly closing time at the shops, because by shopping online people can have access to thousands of shop windows 24 hours a day, 7 days a week. Furthermore, there are no parking problems, or queues at the checkouts. You don't even have to set foot outside your door.

As for the question of prices, there's a veritable price-war going on between online shopping outlets to attract customers and gain their loyalty. All the more so, since the logistics inherent in the Internet (a reduction in stocking costs, no costly high-street rent to pay, no sales assistants, middlemen, etc.) enable them to squeeze prices to the great advantage of the cyber consumer. What's more, the consumers have helpful 'personal shoppers' at their disposal, called ***shopbots*** (shopping robots), which can be used to compare across several outlets the price of a product that a consumer is looking for and so find the best bargain. The advantage of this approach is that you can then take the time to compare the range of products and prices without getting carried away by your initial impulse to buy, or having an over-eager sales assistant breathing down your neck. Last but not least, your purchases will be delivered to your home – no need to struggle back on the bus, or even to your car, with awkwardly shaped packages and dozens of carrier bags.

Of course, this charming picture of the relaxed Internet shopper snapping up bargains at home with the mouse in one hand and a cup of coffee in the other is not completely accurate. Problems can arise – received merchandise not conforming to specification, misleading offers, delivery deadlines not adhered to, orders forgotten, etc. – not to mention the thing that many would-be Internet shoppers fear most nowadays (although it is more psychological than real): credit card fraud. This last risk has been much exaggerated, but it is true that certain precautions are essential, just as with payment in more traditional shopping outlets, or when ordering goods or services by phone.

This book attempts to make good use of the advantages provided by online shopping, by guiding you through the various stages to follow, from hunting out good web addresses and taking advantage of specialist search engines and shopbots, to placing an order and choosing a method of payment. In other words, the book aims to provide you with all the tips you need for successful shopping online. But, to avoid nasty surprises and reduce risks to a minimum, we will also be exploring what your legal rights are, what precautions to take and what redress you can obtain if things go wrong.

Eventually you will see that it is no more dangerous buying things via the Internet than paying for a meal in a restaurant with your credit card.

Throughout this guide, terms shown in ***bold italics*** are somewhat specialised terms that, to aid the reader, are defined in the glossary in Chapter 11.

Finding good addresses

How do you find your way through the thousands of virtual shop windows, and how do you compare their prices to find the best bargain? It's not enough just to hit on the product you're looking for; you still need to know whether the potential purchase is of good quality and value for money. And, given the stiff competition between online businesses, prices can vary by as much as 100 per cent. It's all to the benefit of the consumer, so long as each customer can find the right place in the global *shopping mall* to flush out the most tempting offer.

There are several tools available to help the consumer. Roughly speaking, they can be grouped into three categories:

▸ **search engines** and general information directories, such as SearchUK or Yahoo!;

- *portals* and commercial *shopping directories* – the Internet malls – such as Shoppers Universe or Internet Shopping;

- price-comparison engines – the shopbots – such as Shopping Explorer.

But these categories are reasonably fluid – even inter-changeable – and many sites offer a commercial directory as well as a shopbot. Each is described in more detail below.

Search engines and general directories

You may know of a particular shop or brand name that interests you, and you wonder whether information about it can be found on the Web. If you don't know the **URL** (*Uniform Resource Locator*) or website address, you can try accessing it by putting www. in front of the name (removing any spaces in the name) and .com or co.uk after it. For example, the address of travel agents Thomas Cook is quite simply **www.thomascook.co.uk**.

If this trick doesn't work, the search engines and directories are there to help you. It's best to choose one(s) that you already know how to use (in this same series of books you will find one entitled *Search Engines*, which explains how to use them to best advantage). If you want a company or product of UK origin, use a UK search site or limit your search just to UK sites, as some global engines allow you to do. And don't forget that for a search based on compound words or a series of words, such as the title of a film or a book, it's best to place the sequence of words between quotation marks. Thus, if you want to buy the video of the film *Stand By Me*, you should enter the request 'Stand By Me'.

Alternatively, increasing numbers of engines and directories have a category or channel dedicated to online shopping. Rather than starting a search directly using keywords, it's sometimes more practical first to consult the channel in question and to go on through the headings and subheadings till you reach the product you want. Yahoo! and Excite each offer a pretty comprehensive shopping channel for the UK.

It is preferable to use a search engine rather than a portal or commercial directory (see below) if you're looking for very specific products or manufacturers that are not likely to be listed in a virtual shopping mall designed for mass consumption.

Here are some world-wide search engines to get you started:

Alta Vista

http://www.altavista.com

Google

http://www.google.com

HotBot

http://www.hotbot.com

FAST Search

http://www.alltheweb.com

Northern Light

http://www.northernlight.com

And the following are specific to the United Kingdom:

Excite

http://www.excite.co.uk

SearchUK

http://www.searchuk.com

UK Max

http://www.ukmax.com

UK Plus

http://www.ukplus.com

Yahoo!

http://uk.yahoo.com

Yell

http://www.yell.co.uk

Portals and commercial directories

You're bound to have spent a Saturday wandering around the shops with no particular aim in mind, doing some window shopping just for the fun of it. You can do the same thing on the Web. In fact, there is an increasing number of shopping directories or virtual malls just waiting for you to wander through so they can tempt you with lots of special offers. These virtual shopping malls can include anything from several dozen to several thousand virtual shop-windows.

Most of the malls list online businesses by category (books, computing, electronics, travel, etc.) and sub-categories. Thus, for instance, in the Travel category you should find flights, car rental, holidays, insurance, etc.; in the Computing category you might find hardware, software, accessories, magazines etc. In this way you can select a specific category to find the product you're looking for. Often, you can also search for your product by entering a keyword in the search box of a website's **home page**. Most of the shopping portals don't sell anything themselves and so, for you to make a purchase, a link will usually direct you to the chosen shopping site.

Many of these commercial directories claim to have a selective choice in accordance with criteria such as the reliability of traders, delivery methods or the security of transactions. To learn more about them, click on a link such as **About us**, but bear in mind that it is not always certain that the 'selective choice' offered to customers hasn't been influenced by purely commercial considerations.

One final important remark on this topic: often, the prices displayed do not include the delivery charges, which you only discover when you access the 'shop' itself. Remember this when judging whether or not you are getting value for money for goods or services.

Here are some current portals and directories for you to consider:

2020 Shops

http://www.2020shops.com

A directory based on a strict selection, together with comments and assessments, shopping news and other useful headings. Among the people working for this site there are a number of journalists from the magazine *UK Net*.

BarclaySquare

http://www.barclaysquare.com

Fast and not gimmicky, Barclay Square doesn't list thousands of businesses but aims rather towards quality. Delivery charges are included in the prices displayed and payments are secured.

British Shopping Links

http://www.british-shopping.com

'The UK's Premier Online Shopping Directory' (as it styles itself) enables you to look up the offers of more than 3,000 businesses grouped into 69 categories (antiques, arts, cigars, florists, etc.).

Btspree.com

http://www.btspree.com

The search module enables you to limit your search to the United Kingdom or the United States. *Buying from the USA – a Shopping Guide* gives you all the information you need and the precautions to take when buying from the United States. Dollar prices are converted into pounds sterling.

ESmarts

http://www.esmarts.com

A US directory that offers **hot sites** and **buying guides** for bargain-hunters in various categories: auctions, banks, books, brokers, cars, computers etc. You can also find a list of the 100 most popular shopping sites, as well as information for the consumer. Check carefully whether they deliver your chosen products to the United Kingdom.

The *Guardian*'s Shopping Unlimited

http://www.shoppingunlimited.co.uk

Most of the sites listed here have notes about them, and numerous articles help the buyer to find the right addresses. A good starting point for discovering online shopping, the more so since you can find articles and tools here for online shopping.

Shop Smart

http://www.shopsmart.co.uk

A reputable address for finding bargains in the United Kingdom. Apart from the shopping directory covering more than 2,000 shops online, the Price Comparison Service enables you to compare prices in four categories: books, music, videos/DVDs and computer games. Delivery charges are included in the prices displayed.

Shop@home

http://www.shopathomeuk.com

All the sites listed here are visited and checked to make sure that they run on *secure servers*, among other things. Prices for delivery (standard or express) are also shown.

ShopInParadise

http://www.shopinparadise.co.uk

A selection of more than 6,000 UK shopping sites classified by category: auctions, books, computing, electronic, kids, tickets, etc. There is also access to the Paradise Shopping Network, covering 50 shops.

Shops on the Net

http://www.shopsonthenet.co.uk

A gigantic mall listing more than 8,000 shopping sites. Search by shop, product or category.

Shoppers Universe

http://www.shoppersuniverse.com

If you order a product, Shoppers Universe takes over the transactions without sending you to another shopping site. Security is assured.

Shopbots

Why be limited to a single shop-sign on the Web when the traders offering the same product are legion and prices sometimes vary to an astonishing degree? The reason for not shopping around more, I hear you say, is because that takes a lot of time – and if I do my shopping online, the point is to save time … and money! Now, there is a way to browse around several shop windows in just seconds, and to draw up a table of comparisons for the various offers.

This is where shopbots (shopping robots) come in. Are you looking for a book, a music CD, or some PC software? Using a shopbot, you can specify the product you are looking for, sorted by criteria if relevant (exact model, price range, etc.) and the shopbot brings you a list of prices from different online suppliers, the lowest being at the head of the list. Each price is provided with a link to the shop specified. Then it's up to you to make your choice, without forgetting to check whether the price shown is hiding other extra charges such as VAT or delivery costs.

The general procedure is not at all complicated. You choose a category of products (home electronics, for example), then the type of product (TVs, camcorders, hifi equipment, etc.) and finally the model. Or, if there is a search module and you know the exact model, you can enter it directly into the search box. The shopbot then presents you with a table of comparisons, with the prices offered by the various retailers.

However, you need to realise that these shopbots only cover a defined selection of sites. Is the selection impartial, and does it comply with advertising or commercial agreements? What's more, the selection is relatively limited and, from one shopbot to another, you can discover other shop-signs online. Often, it will be useful to use the services of several shopbots. What is clear is that the technology of shopbots is still developing, and they ought to perform better and better as time goes on.

Shopbots will increase in number over the coming months. So don't be surprised if you don't find the latest arrivals in the (non-exhaustive) selection below. And don't forget that there are still bargains in the high street. There is even a site that explores more than 100 offline retailers to find you the best deals (**http://priceoffers.co.uk**).

A few of the current shopbots are set out next. We start specifically with UK shopbots and end with some from the US, knowing that, although the latter generally cover a much larger number of businesses online, they don't always deliver abroad. It's up to you to check.

Checkaprice

http://www.checkaprice.com

The best deals in different categories and a price-comparison engine for consumers of electronics and household appliances.

DealTime

http://www.dealtime.co.uk

Hundreds of businesses are paraded in different categories: appliances, books, computers, electronics, flowers & gifts, etc. If you're looking for a product that's not listed, you can specify it and DealTime will let you know by e-mail when that product becomes available (through an *e-mail alert*).

MyTaxi

http://www.mytaxi.co.uk

Using the same technology as the US shopbot named Bottom Dollar (see below), My Taxi offers a commercial directory as well as a search tool to find the best prices for books, music and videos. Delivery costs are not included in quoted prices, however.

Kelkoo.com

http://www.shopgenie.co.uk

(Yes, in this case the website address *is* different from the company name.) A very comprehensive site that offers you a search of businesses by country or by categories, as well as buying guides, the best deals of the day, an e-mail alert service and a price comparison for several categories (books, games, toys, consumer electronics, computing, personal finance, etc.).

Pricewatch UK

http://www.euro-pricewatch.com

A price-comparison service for computer hardware, software, CDs, videos, games and books. The service acts as 'Official supporter of the *Which?* Web Trader Code of Practice'. A quick-search box enables you to launch a search covering more than 65,000 prices.

Buy.co.uk

http://www.buy.co.uk

'Cut your bills for dual fuel, electricity, gas, mobiles and water'. You will also find an online shopping directory here.

Pricerunner

http://uk.pricerunner.com

Of Swedish origin, this website is a new arrival on the UK market. Still in an experimental version, it displays astonishing power and compares the prices of a large number of retailers. Present categories include books, computers, home electronics and phones.

My Simon

http://www.mysimon.com

Certainly the most well known for price searches in the US market, it covers a very large number of products. But check that the product you want can be delivered to the United Kingdom.

Bottom Dollar

http://www.bottomdollar.com

Another classic from the United States, also offering a large range of products in many categories.

The Price Guide

http://www.price-guide.co.uk

A price-comparison service for computing, hifi and video equipment, digital cameras, DVD movies, and games. More than 40,000 products and more than 200 suppliers.

3

The buying procedure

After having found a buying site that interests you, scroll through the various categories of products or enter the name or brand of the product you want directly in a 'quick search' box. If the price (inclusive of VAT and delivery) and the conditions of sale (returns policy, guarantee, delivery, etc.) seem worth following up, you can go on to make the purchase itself, after you've made sure the payment system is secure. The ***Help section*** on the website should be able to clarify all these matters for you.

At the side of the photo or description of a specified object for sale, you should find a link such as **Buy Me** or **Add to shopping cart** – the ***cart*** (or shopping basket) in this case being the virtual receptacle in which you place your intended purchases. When you click on the link, a web page normally appears with a confirmation of your order. Check the details on it – particularly the quantity, so that you don't end up with several of the same items. If you want to go on shopping, click the **Back** button or a link that says something like **Return to shopping** or **Continue to shop**.

Remember that the fact that you've put one or more items in your virtual shopping trolley still doesn't commit you in any way to making a purchase. It is only once you have finished your shopping that you need to check the contents of your virtual shopping basket by clicking on a link such as **Update basket** or **View cart**. You can then, if you have changed your mind, reject a purchase by taking it off the list or by reducing the quantity specified to zero. To keep track of what you ordered, save this page to your hard disk or print it out.

Once you have finished shopping you can proceed with the financial transaction to purchase. Click on a link that says something similar to **Go to checkout** or **Continue to secure checkout**. Many online businesses ask you to 'sign up' or 'register' before proceeding with your order, at which point you need to enter the information required, which normally comprises your name, e-mail address and postal address. You are often also asked to choose a username and a password, which you can use for further visits without having to go through the registration process again. After registration, a new web page enables you to specify the delivery address and type of delivery (e.g. Standard or Express) or to choose a gift wrapping, as the case may be. Check the details carefully and continue to the next stage, where you have to reveal your credit- or debit-card details. It is at this stage that you need to be very careful about the information you are entering.

Before entering confidential information, make sure you are on a 'secure' or 'safe' fileserver. In many cases, a message should appear on the screen to warn you that 'You are about to view pages over a secure Internet connection', or something similar. In any case, a closed padlock (or an unbroken key for early Netscape versions) in the bottom toolbar of the window should confirm it. What's more, the address at the top of the window should no longer begins with 'http', but with 'https' (in accordance with the security standard known as *S-HTTP*).

If you are asked for additional personal details, it's up to you whether you answer or not, but you are not obliged to do so. They may simply be requested to help the trader with further marketing, so don't confuse personal details (age, profession, etc.), with confidential information (the PIN of your bank card or your ISP access password, for example), which should not be needed by – and should *never* be given to – anyone else.

Most online businesses then send you an e-mail to confirm your order. Keep this confirmation as well, and make sure that it correctly corresponds with the goods you ordered. Now all you have to do is wait for delivery by the date agreed.

4

The Ten Commandments for the online shopper

Risks are minimal on the Net, whatever people say to the contrary. However, this is not a reason to be slapdash and ignore any of the security rules. Before making a purchase of any kind, always keep in mind the following ten precautionary measures, which will make you a safe shopper. And don't forget that the real world continues to exist, with its high streets, its personal service and its bargains.

1. Ensure the trader is known to you

Whether the trading entity represents a business or a highly-respected brand name, or you know about it by reputation, to identify the trader you should be able to find a link on the home page enabling you to find out the physical location of the organisation and its e-mail address. And don't trust Post Office box numbers as permanent addresses.

If the least doubt crosses your mind, there's nothing to stop you sending the trader a request for information by e-mail. If you don't get a reply, or it comes much too late, go and look elsewhere. Delays are an indication of what might be to come: there is nothing more frustrating than having no one to turn to if there is a problem of any kind with the goods or services you have bought. You could also try phoning any telephone number given to check that it works.

You can also check the identity of who owns the website, through *Who is* (http://www.networksolutions.com/cgi-bin/whois/whois) and thus find out who registered the **domain name** being used by the trader.

2. Check that the transaction is secured

Serious sites must ensure the security of financial transactions through an appropriate technology (**SSL, SET**) and clearly set out for you what their policy is in this regard. If this information cannot be found easily, or if the terms are too vague or appear unfair to the purchaser, don't trust them.

In any case, never send information about your credit card in a non-encrypted form – by e-mail, for example. At the time of the transaction, your details must be transmitted and encrypted through a secure server. How can you be sure of this? By checking for the presence of a closed padlock (or an unbroken key) in the lower part of the browser window and an address starting with 'https' ("s" for secure) instead of 'http'.

If this is not the case and you really want to put in your order, see whether it is possible to transmit your bank details by fax or by telephone (but never by e-mail). Otherwise, forget that address fast!

3. Establish whether the price is all-inclusive

A price that seems attractive at first may turn out not to be if, subsequently, you have to add on delivery costs,

VAT, or customs duties for goods imported from a non-EU country. Be particularly careful in this last case.

Taking all these things into account, it is sometimes more advantageous to buy a product from a local shop that will not charge you anything extra for it.

4. Make sure the terms and conditions of sale are set out clearly

The terms and conditions of the sale must be set out clearly by the trader. Take time to read them carefully from the website before submitting your order. What are the charges you have to pay, the delivery deadlines, the guarantees in case there is a problem? Check out the conditions in detail.

Don't forget that if you buy from a foreign site, delivery dates can be longer and redress for complaints more difficult. If the delivery date is particularly important – for example, you want the goods in time for a birthday – set a limit for the delivery date. And if there is a problem with the goods or services purchased, do not delay: contact the supplier as soon as it is reasonable to do so after the problem comes to light.

5. Avoid impulse buying

The advantage of the Web is that the mouse enables you to go from one shop to another just with a click, and it also gives you an opportunity to compare products and prices. Take advantage of this and don't just jump onto the first 'hot' deal that you encounter; a bit later you might manage a to land on a deal that's less hot – but that is less expensive too.

If there are lots of offers and you are faced with a great deal of choice, print them all out and make your selection with a calm mind. That will prevent you having regrets later.

6. Protect your personal information

Make sure that the retail site follows at least some rules to respect any personal information that it might hold about you. Who can access the information you provide, and for what purpose is it required? A link on the first page of the website – something similar to its ***privacy policy*** or just the Help section – should enable you to find out more. At all costs, provide only the information that is absolutely necessary.

7. Never reveal the PIN code of your credit/debit card

You may think that this is an obvious piece of advice, but it's not a bad idea to be reminded of it from time to time. If anyone asks you for a security number related to bank cards or Internet access, remember you're not in the philanthropy business and change site immediately.

8. Search for traders displaying a standards logo

Traders displaying an appropriate standards logo on their website undertake to comply with a series of specific commercial codes of practice, generally relating to the identification of themselves and their customers, security of transactions, consumer protection, and privacy.

Among those who authorise such logos are *Which?* Web Trader, Direct Marketing Association, TrustUK, WebTrust or ePublicEye. Some will also offer to reimburse you for some of the money you lose if your credit card is misused, for example, *Which?* .

Their websites are:

http://www.which.net/webtrader/index.html

http://www.the-dma.org

http://www.trustuk.org.uk

http://www.webtrust.net

http://www.thepubliceye.com

9. Check the terms of the returns or goodwill policy

Errors do sometimes occur so that you could end up with a product that you didn't order or that does not correspond exactly with what you specified. Before putting in an order, make sure you are clearly covered for this type of irritating occurence (see Commandment 4). Over and above this type of cover, many sites offer a *goodwill policy*. This can enable you to exchange an item that is not to your liking, even though it is in line with what you ordered and you have no redress as part of your legal rights.

And don't forget that a 1999 European Directive on remote selling is very explicit on the subject of consumer protection (page 106).

10. Keep the proof of your order

Take a screen print or other printout, or make a disk copy, of anything that proves you made the order and your online purchase – this is of prime importance. If a problem were to arise, you would at least have proof of the transaction and thus have a chance of obtaining redress. It is wise to follow this process systematically whenever you make any Internet transaction.

If you are concerned about running up a big bill while ambling around the shops on the Internet in a virtual kind of way, try shopping offline. Once you have decided what you want to buy, you simply go online to place your order. This works by using the temporary files that your browser stores on your hard disk as you browse. These are known as *cache* in Netscape and *Temporary Internet Files* in Internet Explorer. Go to the **File** menu and select **Go offline** or **Work offline**. Then access a site by typing in the address, or following links as if you were online. Note that the temporary files will only store the pages for a certain time and will be overwritten the next time you visit the same site.

5

Auctions,
co-buying,
and classified ads

Auctions

Hardly had they appeared on the Net than online auctions very quickly triggered an unprecedented deluge of bids, with bidding sites proliferating in every country. They already represent a not inconsiderable part of e-commerce, and the phenomenon continues to grow. The thrill of competing in an auction, the excitement of winning it and obtaining an object for a, hopefully, ridiculous price have led many Internet users to become devotees of these virtual auction rooms.

You can find just about anything, as if the auction site were a gigantic flea-market: from the latest gadgets to uniforms from the 1914–18 war, from paintings by old masters to a casino slot-machine, from a 1949 bottle of port to a Pokémon collection, and so on. For instance, on the e-Bay site alone (see page 62), there are as many as 4 million items for which you can bid. Imagine even the most bizarre of items and there is a good chance that you'll find it in an auction, not least because they are world-wide. You can go from one auction sale in New Zealand to another in the United States to another in Germany, taking into account the differing time zones round the world.

How auctions work

Online auctions operate very logically. Mr X wants to get rid of his camcorder. He goes to an auction site and offers the object there, displaying its technical features accompanied by a photo. Some sites offer to scan the photo for you. Sites also include information about conditions of sale, such as the starting price for bids, the reserve price (below which the object may not be sold), the methods of payment and delivery, and the closing date. Mr X then waits for the bids, hoping that they will go above his wildest expectations.

The highest bid at the closing date will gain the object (subject to the bid being at least the reserve price), which explains why it is often at the last minute that people get carried away, each bidder being ready to overbid in order to acquire some coveted object. You can enter the bidding at any time 'in person', although some sites also offer a system of automatic bidding whereby you decide your top limit and the system bids on your behalf in the lowest possible increments. If you win the auction, you will receive an e-mail confirming the fact. Sale periods often last a week, but there are also 'impulse auctions' that last only a few hours.

Most of the auction sites currently running on the Internet do nothing more than put individual sellers and buyers into contact with each other. Generally speaking, the seller will pay a listing fee (£1, for example) and a percentage of the sale price (from 2.5 to 5 per cent), while the buyer will pay nothing except the sale price and delivery charges. Other sites sell directly – things like stock returns, surpluses, etc.

When buying directly from a site, you have a little more protection as you pay with a credit card, unlike when buying from a private individual. You therefore have the protection that the credit card normally affords you. Nevertheless, you should still make checks on the site to make sure that it is a reputable one, as described on page 57.

To take part in auctions, you are first asked to register, giving your address, telephone number and other necessary information. You will then receive a password, which you will have to enter each time you place a bid. Some sites, such as QXL (see page 63), also ask you for your credit card details to ensure that, when you have to pay for a successful bid, the payment is guaranteed. Read the conditions carefully for participating in an auction, as these can vary from one site to another. As soon as you make a bid, you are automatically acknowledging that you have read and agreed to these conditions. Don't expect the site to intervene in case of problems; these have to be sorted out directly between seller and buyer.

Consumer's rights are far fewer when buying at auction than when buying in another manner. It is a system that operates more on trust and you enter into a legal contract with the seller. To help avoid difficulties, you can make use of a system to ensure the security of the transaction, which is called an *escrow* service. The seller and the buyer register with a trustworthy third party, who receives the specified sum from the buyer. Once the object has been delivered and is to the satisfaction of the buyer, the latter informs the service, which then pays the seller. QXL uses such a service, and there are specialist companies that provide this type of secured transaction, such as i-Escrow (http://www.iescrow.com), I Trust You (http://www.itrustyou.com) and TradeSafe (http://www.tradesafe.com). There's nothing to stop you suggesting this type of intermediary to sellers, even if some of them refuse.

Some advice

Here are some other words of advice to bear in mind if you plan to get involved in online – and real-life – auctions:

▸ The start-price seems so trifling (and that's the point!) that you don't hesitate for a moment to jump in and place a bid. With excitement driving you on, you may be tempted to offer a price that you would never pay under calmer circumstances. So keep your cool, or you may end up paying far more than you intended. Before you start, work out the maximum price you want to pay and beyond which you will not go. Also, remember that if you make the winning bid you are legally obliged to buy; you cannot then change your mind, just as at a 'real' auction.

▸ Check out the site's privacy policy. An auction site can acquire quite a bit of personal information about you, for example, the kind of products in which you are interested. They could sell this on to marketing companies, who may only use it to bombard you with unwanted mailings, but nevertheless, this is an invasion of your privacy. Look for privacy seals such as the TRUSTe seal, which indicate that the site undertakes to comply with privacy guidelines.

▸ Before taking part in an auction, find out the usual value of the object if you can (especially for collectibles) and study all the details displayed carefully, so that you don't get any surprises when it is delivered.

▸ You can often find consumer 'reviews', written by people who have already taken part in a particular auction, relating their experience and how successful, or otherwise, it was. If you can't find any information about the seller, try sending an e-mail asking for physical details (such as identity, address, and phone number) or additional information on the object being put up for auction. You will then have information helping you to obtain redress if a problem occurs.

▸ After making a purchase, you could also take part in making an assessment of the seller, whether positive or negative. This is how buyers can help each other and prevent disagreeable experiences for others.

▸ If you buy electronic or other equipment, remember that the guarantee supplied when the equipment was new may no longer be valid. Is it worth the risk?

▸ Before paying, make sure both you and the seller are perfectly clear about the delivery details (costs, deadlines). Never send cash. Be wary of anyone who ask you to do so. At most, if necessary, pay cash on delivery.

▶ Ask the seller to send the goods via an insured secure method, such as registered mail or courier, though you will have to pay the cost of this. However, if there is any damage in transit you should be able to make an insurance claim.

Auction websites

Amazon.co.uk

http://www.amazon.co.uk

Amazon also offers an auction section for books, music, films and electronics. For some videos and DVDs, bidding starts at just £1. A link at the bottom of the home page will take you there.

Aucland

http://www.aucland.co.uk

Thousands of items classified by category and a free insurance scheme through the Axa insurance company.

Auction Guide

http://www.auctionguide.com

For finding auctions throughout the world (both online and offline). You can search by category (antiques, arts, computer, household, jewellery, etc.) or by continent.

Auction Connect

http://www.auctionconnect.lycos.com

Are you looking for a particular item? This service undertakes to find it for you on the major auction sites.

Auction Net

http://www.auctions.co.uk

'Your Internet resource for UK auctions' classified by categories (art and antiques, cars and motor vehicles, catering equipment, computer, general, property).

BidnBuy

http://www.bidnbuy.com

Auction site for the sale of computer products, peripherals and consumer electronics.

eBay

http://www.ebay.com

A veritable 'Aladdin's cave', with literally millions of items of all kinds. The UK site (http://www.ebay.co.uk) offers a more reduced choice, but with fewer delivery problems.

eBid

http://www.eBid.co.uk

Another well-stocked auction site. It offers a SafePay and SafeShip service.

Eurobid

http://www.eurobid.com

Auctions on a European scale. You pay in euros or a local currency.

Fired Up

http://www.firedup.com

This site gives access to a very wide choice of goods of all kinds and attractive offers.

Go Ricardo

http://www.goricardo.co.uk

All categories are listed here: antiques, books, collectibles, computer, films, house & garden, etc.

QXL

http://www.qxl.co.uk

A reference site for auctions in the United Kingdom. It has the SafePay/SafeShip security system for transactions, and QXL provides a useful guide for those starting out on the auction adventure for the first time.

Yahoo! auctions

http://uk.auctions.yahoo.com/uk

Another very active site for auctions in the United Kingdom.

Reverse auctions

Something that originated in the US, this is a new style of auction where buyers indicate what they want to buy and how much they are prepared to pay, and then sit back and let traders and suppliers compete for their business. There is no reason why you should not be able to buy the same items that you can buy in conventional Web shopping in this way, from televisions and video recorders to flights and insurance. Your requirements are sent to a site that will then sort and forward your request to appropriate suppliers, who will then respond. There are already a number of sites, offering retail goods (eg.**www.ybag.com**), financial services (eg. **www.moneysupermarket.com** for mortgage lenders) or flights (eg.**www.priceline.co.uk**).

Co-buying

There's strength in numbers, as the saying goes, and this concept is a good illustration of this particular type of group purchasing on the Web. Co-buying, group buying, aggregate buying – there are various terms to describe a very simple principle.

The larger the quantity purchased, the lower the price. Traders or purchasing centres have profited from this rule for a very long time. But, in the case of electronic purchasing, it's the consumers who will benefit from it, thanks to the Web. If fifty people each buy a DVD player, they will each be at the usual market price. If these same fifty people get together and make their purchase together as one, they acquire purchasing power that enables them to obtain a discounted price for each player. Generally speaking, the greater the number of buyers, the lower the price will fall. So it is very much in the interests of every buyer to get together with friends and acquaintances to increase the number of items purchased.

The co-buying method of purchase started in the United States and, since then, numerous sites in Europe have adopted the same approach. It's a system that is bound to grow with the continuing increase in the number of Internet shoppers. This approach is the opposite of that used in auctions, where each person has only one desire – to outdo the others. Co-buying is all about team spirit – not just e-commerce but '*we-commerce*'!

The offers available by means of co-buying are extremely varied. From designer-lamps to a weekend in a three-star hotel, via home cinema, fridges, palmtop computers or solar-powered short-wave radio – there's something here for everyone's tastes. Several sites even offer to take up your own suggestions for group purchasing.

How it works

You can browse for a product or search for it by category or keyword on a co-buying site. The offers are found in **buy-cycles**. A time limit is put on the cycle and a certain number of buyers are required to get through various stages up to the 'target price' (or 'best price'). For example, Letsbuyit (see below) was offering a DVD player for sale the average retail price of which was £279. This price dropped to £240 for 1–3 buyers, to £229 for 4–7 buyers, and the best price, £219, for 8–30 players. In that particular co-buying cycle, the price reached its lowest because there were 13 buyers.

To co-buy, you normally have to register and open an account using a username and password (but without the details of your bank card). Then to purchase a product, you have to join the buy-cycle. There are two options available to you. You can either agree to buy the item at the current price, with the chance of seeing the price drop subsequently when other buyers come in, enabling you to benefit also from the lower price. Or you can agree to buy the item only if the best price is reached, with the risk that it might not fall that far if the required number of buyers is not reached, in which case you don't make the purchase. In collective buying, each person pays the lowest price reached and no more.

Payment is made at the end of the buy-cycle and not before. An e-mail will inform you of the price obtained and your financial commitment.

Some advice

Here are some further words of advice to bear in mind if you plan to get involved in co-buying arrangements:

- Clearly, it is tempting to get a bargain by making a saving of say 30 per cent on the normal retail price. However, before you commit, visit a few other sites, or take a trip down the high street, to check what the current price really is. You can sometimes be surprised.

- Before getting caught up in co-buying, carefully read all the information about the product in question and keep a copy of it.

- Watch out for hidden costs. Are VAT and delivery charges included in the price, or extra to be added on?

- Just as for any other purchase, check what the seller's returns policy and guarantee are.

- Most co-buying sites offer a secured payment system. But make sure of it.

▶ If, after you've made all your checks, you are sure that this is a real bargain, tell your friends about it. You'll be doing them a favour, as well as yourself.

Co-buying websites

Adabra

http://www.adabra.com

Tends to concentrate on electrical goods.

LetsBuyIt

http://www.letsbuyit.com/en_GB/

Represented in 14 countries, this Swedish group targets a Europe-wide purchasing community and has more than 800,000 members. A trip to Sydney Australia, a micro-skate scooter, a Suzuki motocross bike – you'll find a bit of everything. Search by category or by product.

MobShop

http://www.mobshop.co.uk

This site specialises in computer hardware, electronics, mobile telephony and PDAs (Personal Digital Assistants – small hand-held computers where the user writes on a screen with a stylus). Hot buy-cycles of the day and free UK delivery.

UnionDream

http://www.uniondream.com/GB_en

Represented in several European countries, Union-Dream offers a large assortment of products and brands (Philips, Psion, Slazenger, Creative Labs, Burley, etc.). Search by category, by brand name or by keyword. If you don't find the product of your dreams, Dreambox awaits your suggestions.

Classifieds

The Internet is particularly suited to searching classified advertisement lists. The sites or sections dedicated to them enable you to find what you want, searching by heading, region or keyword. You'll find everything in the classifieds, from attic 'treasures' to second-hand cars, properties in Spain to cameras, last-minute flights to electric guitars. What's more, e-mail easily puts you in contact with a seller so that you can get the information you want.

Most of the portals and search engines have their own section for classified ads, but you can also find specialist sites. Some of them also offer exchange services; thus you might find someone who wants to exchange his house in Gloucester for an Alfa-Romeo. But be careful, because you have little legal protection in this type of transaction. And it is preferable to choose sellers from your own region, as then you can go and check the condition of the item you are considering and delivery or collection should be much more manageable.

Classified ad websites

Autotrader

http://www.autotrader.co.uk

Exchange and Mart

http://www.exchangeandmart.co.uk

Fish4

http://www.fish4.co.uk

Local Ads

http://www.localads.net

London Free Exchange

http://london.freeexchange.co.uk

Loot

http://www.loot.com

Photo Ads

http://www.photoads.co.uk

Preloved

http://www.preloved.co.uk

WebCity

http://www.webcity.co.uk

Webswappers

http://www.webswappers.com

Yahoo! Classifieds

http://uk.classifieds.yahoo.com/uk

6

Buying from abroad

Buying from sites abroad enables you to find things you can't get in your own home. The Web has no national frontiers and, with online shopping, that situation opens up all the businesses of the world to you. However, there are some potential drawbacks to overcome.

You need to establish early on that a supplier situated abroad will deliver to your location. Although it is sometimes possible through the Internet to find the same goods abroad at a lower price than at which they are available at home, the deal may not be quite as good as it appears at first sight. You should always take into account (especially in relation to the United States) the cost of delivery charges, taxes and customs duties. There can be additional complications if a problem arises to do with the goods themselves or their delivery. You would not want to have to send back defective items at your own expense.

It's a good idea to get information in advance from sites or organisations dealing with consumer protection about a particular site from which you intend to buy, and to let them know about the reliability of Web shops you have used. Thus, BizRate (**http://www.bizrate.com**) or ePublicEye (**http://www.thepubliceye.com**) reference the US shopping sites in accordance with very specific criteria. And, similar to the *Which?* Webtrader in the United Kingdom, the Better Business Bureau (**http://www.bbb.com**) provides a good-conduct label for certain US shopping sites if they adhere to a series of definite rules.

In any case, don't waste time (and money) surfing foreign sites to find a bargain without undertaking certain special precautions. Let's have a look at them next.

Technical compatibility

Finding the latest piece of equipment at a bargain price on the Web is all very well, but not such a good idea if you cannot use it. If you were to buy a video recorder or a TV from the United States, all you would see when plugged in at home would be an empty screen as the standards for image transmission are not the same in Europe (PAL/SECAM) and the United States (NTSC). The same applies to video cassettes: be sure to check they are in a format compatible with your equipment.

DVDs are encoded according to geographical zones (Zone 1 for the United States, Zone 2 for Europe, etc.) and your DVD player may not be able to read DVDs purchased in the States. Having said that, some DVDs are not encoded and some players can read DVDs from different zones. So be careful and, before buying, check the zone of the DVD and the capabilities of your player. As far as CDs or CD-ROMs are concerned, there's no problem: they are recognised by all players.

If you buy a piece of electrical equipment abroad, make sure that it doesn't operate on a different voltage from your home country. If it does, you will need a transformer.

If you have any doubts, ask the seller to confirm the compatibility of the item before you buy and save this confirmation just in case.

One last but less technical point: the sizes of clothes. Measurement systems are far from universal. However, many sites offer a size comparison chart where you can find the equivalent of your own measurements.

Additional charges

▶ **Delivery arrangements**

After making sure that the seller does indeed deliver abroad and to your home country, don't forget the delivery charges. Some shopping sites are not very clear on this subject, and sometimes you have to spend too much time finding the information you want. Is the purchase still worth the trouble? Will it be delivered on time (for a birthday, for example)?

▶ **Taxes and customs duties within the European Union**

Any purchase made within the European Union is free of customs duties, but you will have to pay VAT (charged and collected by the seller), except for certain items such as books, children's clothes or food. For alcohol and tobacco, you have to pay both excise duty and VAT. For your searches on European shopping websites, you can consult the directory (in French) of HotWin (http://www.hotwin.com). Furthermore, for French sites alone there are lots of other directories available: for instance, AcheterNet (http://www.acheter.net) and Promoselect (http://www.promoselect.com) – not forgetting the national versions of Yahoo! or Excite, for example.

▸ **Taxes and customs duties outside the European Union**

Any purchase made outside the EU is subject to any or all of three charges: customs duty, excise duty and VAT, unless the goods are worth less than £18 including delivery charges. The exceptions to this rule are tobacco, alcohol, perfume and toilet waters, where duty applies whatever the value of the goods. Though VAT is fixed at 17.5 per cent in most cases in the United Kingdom, duty rates vary considerably from item to item: 14 per cent for a DVD player, 3.5 per cent for an audio CD or 12 per cent for shirts. You will find all the details concerning this question on the UK Customs and Excise site (http://www.hmce.gov.uk).

▶ **Total due**

To work out how much an imported item is going to cost you, a little calculation is in order. First add the delivery charge to the cost of the item. Then multiply this sum by the duty rate, then by the VAT rate. As an example, let's take an order for £94.05 for CDs from India, with a delivery charge of £5.95 on top, making £100.00 exactly. Adding 3.5 per cent customs duty gives us a running total of £103.50. This sum is then multiplied by the UK VAT rate for CDs of 17.5 per cent, which comes to £18.11. The total now comes to £103.50 + £18.11, or £121.61. So the additional costs, on top of the CDs, come to £5.95 for delivery and £21.61 for tax and duty.

▶ **Paying the tax and duty**

In theory, you have to pay the duty and tax due (in the foregoing example, an extra £21.61) to the postman when he delivers the goods. The company selling the goods is required to label them, giving the value and type of goods, so that the Post Office can calculate the amount due. The Post Office may also charge you for clearing your package through customs; i.e. handling packages for customs examination and opening and repackaging them if necessary. So you could be charged both the handling fee and the duty/excise/VAT.

But, in reality, collecting these taxes is rather haphazard and in many cases the Post Office does not claim any payment from you.

▶ **Goods supplied electronically**

Digitised products (for example, software and music clips) which are ordered and delivered electronically over the Net (i.e. that you download) are free of customs and excise duties as they are treated as services. However, you still have to pay VAT when they are bought from within the EU, though it is hard to see how this could be collected. If they are supplied from outside the EU, they are free of VAT.

7

Payment
and security

The credit or debit card is the most common form of payment on the Net, and, despite popular belief, the safest provided the guidelines on security are adhered to. The great majority of online businesses use a system called Secure Sockets Layer (SSL) or SET, based on an encryption technology that makes it possible to ensure the confidentiality of transactions and hides your credit card details from any disreputable prying eyes on the Net. You should buy from only those businesses that adhere to these payment-security standards.

A company that wishes to set up a secure site has to apply for a certificate of *authentication*. To receive this it has to provide proof that it is who it claims to be. When visiting a secure site, the web server sends a signal to your web browser asking it to switch to secure mode. The server then sends its certificate of authentication in the form of a series of numbers, which then ensures that the information you transmit over the Web is scrambled, just like in an old spy film! A hacker could still hack into or intercept the information but would not be able to read it.

If you land on a site that, when you are making a transaction, asks you to fill in a form and send it by e-mail, don't do this under any circumstances. E-mail is not encrypted during transmission and can easily be intercepted by a hacker. Instead, if it's possible, send your details by phone or fax, as a number of sites allow you to do.

When you go into secure mode, a Security Alert message may appear on your computer screen to advise you of this. You should see an unbroken key (for the older versions of Netscape) or a closed padlock at the bottom of the screen and the address will no longer begin with 'http' but with 'https'. Another way of ensuring that you're in secure mode is to click with the right mouse button on the form you have to fill in. Choose Properties from the menu and you will be able to see whether your connection is secure or not.

So, you have several means at your disposal to check whether you are in secure mode and whether it's safe to submit your order, but, if you have the slightest doubt, hold back. Only go ahead with your order if you have found information about the website that fully satisfies your uncertainties (in the Help section, for example).

You may find that, for purchases under a certain sum, you cannot pay by credit or debit card. This is because the charges the card companies make to process the transactions would be too expensive for the seller in relation to the cost of the item. This is where digital cash or an ***electronic wallet*** comes in handy. You register with a provider who sets up a 'wallet' that contains your bank details and issues you with a security code. You simply type in your security code when you wish to buy something and the seller charges the cost to your wallet. However, you may find that not all sellers participate in this scheme. See page 93 for some relevant websites.

Payment cards

If you find the different types of 'plastic' money confusing, here is a quick run down on the different types of card:

▸ **Credit cards**

Examples of some of the big names are Mastercard and Visa. Most sites will accept payment by credit card and you will have some additional security (see *If there's a problem*, page 94). When the monthly credit card bill arrives, you can pay it off in full, in which case there is no extra charge, or you can choose to pay off a proportion, but in that case you will be charged interest on the outstanding balance.

▸ **Debit cards**

These cards are issued by your bank or building society. When paying with this type of card the money will be taken out of your bank or building society directly, with no period of credit. It therefore functions in a similar way to a cheque drawn on your account.

▸ **Charge cards**

An example of this kind of card is American Express. It functions in a similar way to a credit card as payment is not demanded of you immediately, but when the bill does arrive, payment must be made in full.

▶ **Store cards**

These are supplied by individual department stores, e.g. Marks and Spencer or John Lewis. You should be able to use store cards when visiting the store's own site, but not elsewhere on the Net.

A few electronic wallet addresses:

http://www.mastercard.com/shoponline/e-wallets
http://www.trivnet.com
http://www.instabuy.com
http://www.passport.com
http://www.barclay.co.uk

If there's a problem...

Buying something with a credit card (but not with a debit or charge card) gives you certain rights. For items costing between £100 and £30,000 (with a total credit value of less than £25,000) the credit card issuer is jointly liable with the seller if there is a problem with goods or services. You can therefore make a claim against the card company instead of the seller. You can also claim for inconsequential loss, i.e. if something you buy over the Internet is faulty and damages something else as a result. This is a useful recourse if, for example, the seller goes bankrupt or disappears into thin air before the merchandise is delivered.

For further information take a look at section 75 of the UK's Consumer Credit Act 1974, the details of which you will find on the site of the Office of Fair Trading (http://www.oft.gov.uk). Furthermore, several online businesses (Amazon or BOL, for example) undertake to reimburse your liability as well if the loss occurred during a transaction with them.

Viruses

This advice really applies to all areas of the Internet, not just shopping. A computer virus is a dastardly thing that can spread from one computer to another, corrupting files, erasing parts of your hard disk and generally causing havoc. After the world-wide devastation wreaked by the infamous Love Bug during 2000, it would be as well to take the precaution of installing antivirus protection software. It is possible to download free software directly from the Internet.

Privacy

You can browse through a shopping site without having to enter any personal information about yourself, but if you do want to buy anything you have to register, giving at least your name and e-mail address. Before you do so, it is a good idea to check that the site has a ***privacy policy***, normally listed in the Help section. The site should say that it will not pass on your details to another party or send you unsolicited mail.

When you visit a website it places a ***cookie***, or small text file, on the hard disk of your computer. This enables the website to keep track of your shopping habits and has its pros and cons. It will mean that you don't have to go through the same setting-up procedure the next time you visit the site, but on the other hand you may not appreciate the fact that the site knows all about your penchant for Belgian chocolates and Kylie Minogue CDs as soon as you visit it. Cookies also give traders marketing information and help them target their sites appropriately.

8

Your rights as
a consumer

For many people, the Internet is still a jungle, a Wild West beyond the reach of any law or regulations. But it's not really like that, particularly as far as online shopping is concerned. The online consumer is not unprotected – quite the contrary. In the UK the consumer has the same rights regarding items bought over the Internet as those bought in the high street or other conventional outlets. Make sure you know what your rights are and how to use them should the need arise, which should only happen very rarely provided you observe a minimum of prudence. It's worth knowing them, particularly since they apply to purchasing both online and offline.

Here are their main points, but for further information and advice visit the site of the Office of Fair Trading (http://www.oft.gov.uk). Don't forget, however, that these rights are applicable in the UK only. If you are buying something from abroad, you don't enjoy the same level of protection and if something goes wrong you may find yourself very exposed and without recourse to any form of protection other than the trader's goodwill. See also 'The European Union Distance Selling Directive' page 106.

What UK law says

The law in the United Kingdom stipulates that goods must fulfil certain criteria. They must be:

▸**as described** – on the website. If you are told a shirt is 100 per cent cotton, then that is what it should be and not, for example, a mixture of polyester and cotton.

▸**of satisfactory quality** – the goods must meet the standard that a reasonable person would regard as acceptable, bearing in mind the way they were described, what they cost and any other relevant circumstances. This covers, for instance, the appearance and finish of the goods, their safety and their durability. Goods must be free from defects – even minor ones – except when the flaws have been brought to your attention by the seller (for example, if the goods are said to be 'shop-soiled' or 'factory seconds').

▶ **fit for their purposes**, including any particular purpose mentioned by you to the seller – for example, if you are buying a computer game and you explain that you want one that can be played on a particular type of machine, the seller must not supply you with one that is incompatible with your machine, provided you explained this requirement to him.

These are your UK statutory rights – rights enshrined in law chiefly through the Sale of Goods Act 1979. All goods bought over the Internet are covered by these rights. A new item must look new and unspoiled as well as work properly, but if the goods are second-hand, or 'factory seconds' and are described as such, then you cannot expect perfect quality.

Furthermore, you have no real grounds to complain if you:

▸ were told about a specific fault;
▸ did the damage yourself;
▸ made a mistake when purchasing an item;
▸ simply changed your mind about an item.

Under these circumstances, you are not legally entitled to anything, but traders may help you out of goodwill. It is always worth asking.

If there's a problem ..

If something goes wrong with the transaction or soon afterwards:

If there is something wrong with what you buy, tell the seller as soon as possible. It is a good idea to e-mail or phone to let them know about your com-

plaint. Make a written note of a phone conversation or take a copy of e-mail correspondence.

If you tell the seller promptly that the goods are faulty and you do not want them, you should be able to get your money back. As long as you have not legally accepted the goods, you can still reject them – that is, refuse to accept them. One of the ways you accept goods is by keeping them, without complaint, after you have had a reasonable time to examine them. What is reasonable is not fixed; it depends on all the circumstances. But normally you can at least try your purchase out at home. If, however, you delay in examining what you have bought, or in telling the seller about a fault, then you may lose your right to reject.

Note that if you signed an acceptance note on receiving goods, this does not mean you have signed away your right to reject. You still have a reasonable time to examine them.

So if, after delivery, you discover that something you've bought is defective, you are entitled to a full refund. If you accept that the trader will repair it for you or replace it, let him know in writing that you reserve the right to refuse it if it still does not comply with your rights as they are defined (use the phrase 'without prejudice' in your communication).

If the problem persists and before resorting to other forms of redress, explain clearly to the seller the reason for your complaint with as much information about it as possible (date of order, description of the item ordered, amount and method of payment, precise reasons for the complaint, etc.). Keep copies of any correspondence safe.

If you are still unable to resolve your differences with the seller, there are a few addresses on the following page that could be useful to you.

Citizens Advice Bureau

http://www.nacab.org.uk

Consumers Association

http://www.which.com

Office of Fair Trading

http://www.oft.gov.uk

Advertising Standards Association

http://www.asa.org.uk

Trading Standards (central)

http://www.tradingstandards.gov.uk

Internet Consumer Assistance Bureau

http://www.isitsafe.com

Direct Marketing Association

http://www.dma.org.uk

The European Union Distance Selling Directive

This EU Directive, which should come into effect on the 31st of October, is designed to give extra protection to consumers in the European Union. It applies expressly to electronic commerce and other forms of distance selling and covers most goods and services sold via the Net, with the exception of financial services.

Here are its main points:

- The consumer must have precise information, such as the address and identity of the seller, the main characteristics of the goods or services, and the price of goods or services including taxes and delivery charges.

- The consumer must receive written confirmation of the order, though in practice this will generally accompany the goods on delivery.

▸ The consumer must have a period of seven days after receipt of the goods in which to change his or her mind, and this period extends to three months if the information obligation (first bullet point) has not been fulfilled.

▸ The order must be executed within 30 days if, at the time of conclusion of the purchase, no delivery date has been agreed. If the article for sale is not available, the sum paid by the consumer must be reimbursed.

It should be noted that these stipulations do not apply to financial services, nor CDs, videos, food, newspapers or magazines.

If you have a problem with goods ordered from within the EU, you can contact a Euroguichet office, financed by the European Commission to provide information on how to resolve EU cross-border consumer complaints. Again, check out the Office of Fair Trading's website (http://www.oft.gov.uk).

Other (non-statutory) rights

In addition to the statutory rights described above, a number of traders offer you the benefit of their goodwill policies. It's up to you to check what further rights they grant you. Thus, some of them allow you to exchange an article that you are not satisfied with, even when they are not legally obliged to do so.

You should also check what the manufacturer's guarantee is, and don't forget to return the guarantee registration document duly completed. Any such guarantee grants you additional protection, but it is separate from the seller's obligations. According to the law, it is the seller who is responsible for defective goods and he may not offload that responsibility onto the manufacturer.

Be careful when buying abroad. The product guarantee is not necessarily valid in another country. Thus, if you buy a laptop in the United States and a problem arises subsequently, you will have to send it back to the United States at your own expense to have it repaired. The saving you thought you were making initially could turn out to be very expensive. So, make sure you have the relevant information beforehand, especially if you are buying electronic equipment.

At auctions

The rights set out above apply to purchases made from an online business, but not to auctions. These are based on a relationship of tacit trust between the seller and buyer, and a website running an auction is not responsible for what goes on between the two parties (unless it explicitly undertakes such responsibility and offers certain guarantees). So you must be very cautious indeed when you bid in online auctions.

Get as much information as you can on the article you want to buy – its condition, age, etc. Try also to find out as much as possible about the seller since, clearly, you are buying from a completely unknown source. Many auction sites try to help in this regard by offering a 'review' system where sellers are rated by buyers for efficiency, returns policy, whether the goods match the description, etc.

Check too whether the seller offers other identification information and not just an e-mail address. It is always more reassuring to have a physical address and a telephone number. See also the general advice on buying at auction starting on page 57.

9

Directory
of addresses

In this section you will find a selection of addresses, classified by category of products. This selection is not exhaustive – far from it – but that is not the purpose of this guide. The addresses given will enable you to make a start with your shopping online and to discover some of the Internet's better-known shop windows.

Don't forget that, in Chapter 2 on 'Finding good addresses', you will find a number of basic pointers (directories, shopbots, search engines, etc.) for exploring the virtual shopping mall that is growing from day to day. Good hunting!

Books and magazines

The sale of books is without doubt the sector that has exploded the fastest in e-shopping. Amazon was one of the pioneers, but, since then, competition has grown and no bookshop in the world can provide the breadth of choice you now have on the Net. Best-sellers, scientific books, children's books, rare or second-hand books – virtually everything is available and often at very competitive prices. It is not uncommon to find best-sellers at 50 per cent of their official price. In addition, websites have a number of useful aspects, offering book lists, readers' reviews and ratings, interviews with authors, bibliographies, etc.

Don't forget that, as with many items, delivery will cost you less if you buy several books together instead of one at a time.

General book suppliers

Alphabetstreet

http://www.alphabetstreet.co.uk

An enormous choice of books in different categories, and price reductions from 20 to 50 per cent of high-street prices. If you are out of ideas, consult the Recommendations Gizmo.

Amazon

http://www.amazon.co.uk

An outstanding reference site in this field with an enormous and unbeatable choice, a powerful search module, and reductions of 50 per cent on best-sellers. Interviews with authors, critical reviews, and a gift service.

Barnes & Noble

http://www.barnesandnoble.com

This American chain of bookstores is a serious competitor for Amazon. It has an enormous selection, and reductions of 50 per cent on best-sellers.

BOL.com

http://www.uk.bol.com

This is the book supermarket developed by the Bertelsman empire. Promotions, recommendations, critical reviews, personalisation service and a next-day delivery option (at additional cost). This company also has a CD section.

The Country Bookshop

http://www.countrybookshop.co.uk

An independent bookshop that is doing well. It offers books at bargain prices (up to 80 per cent discount), a free gift-wrapping service, an out-of-print search service, and possibilities for exchange or reimbursement.

The Internet Bookshop

http://www.bookshop.co.uk

The online version of W.H. Smith offers more than 1.4 million book titles at any one time. Special entries in the website on new issues, interviews and critical reviews. They also have CDs, videos and games for sale.

Ottakars'

http://www.ottakars.co.uk

Online version of the chain that has a good range of titles, plus recommendations, competitions and offers. A site that has the added benefit of being easy to use.

Waterstone's

http://www.waterstones.co.uk

This site too offers a very wide choice, with the possibility of personalisation and searches for items that are out of print. Free delivery to your nearest Waterstone's branch and exchange possibilities are other aspects of the service offered.

Specialist suppliers

BookFinder

http://www.bookfinder.com

A search engine to help you find a second-hand book from various independent booksellers.

BookLovers

http://www.booklovers.co.uk

Quality second-hand books searchable by author, title or keyword. You can sell books here too.

Books for Children

http://freespace.virgin.net/books-for.children

A limited selection of books for children, classified by age (0–2, 2–4, 4–6).

British Magazines Direct

http://www.britishmagazines.com

More than 3,500 magazines classified by theme (computer

and Internet, women's interests, business, cooking, music, etc.), which can be purchased by number or by subscription.

Computer Manuals Online Bookstore

http://www.compman.co.uk

A very wide choice covering all computer sectors. The company's returns policy enables you to exchange a book you're not satisfied with.

Magazineshop

http://www.magazineshop.co.uk

A very wide choice of magazines, but by subscription only. 'The lowest subscription rates available.'

Maps Worldwide

http://www.mapsworldwide.co.uk

More than 10,000 maps, guides and atlases. Topographical maps, road maps, satellite images, …

Clothes and accessories

Sales of clothing by postal catalogue have been in existence for a long time now. So it's not surprising that the Web displays numerous shop windows in this sector. From small boutiques to large chain-stores, from the inevitable T-shirts to the latest trends, the choice is growing from day to day, for men, women and children.

It may be stating the obvious, but the disadvantage is that you cannot try anything on and sizes are not standardised, varying from manufacturer to manufacturer, not to mention from country to country.   Therefore check out whether or not a company will allow you to return goods free of charge, or you risk costly postal charges, particularly to another country.

America's Shirt Catalogue

http://www.hugestore.com

Top US clothes at discount rates: shirts, of course, but also casual trousers, jeans, ties, sports coats and other items.

The Arcadia Group

http://www.arcadiagroup.co.uk

A group of shops offering well-known brands: Burton, Evans, Dorothy Perkins, Principles, Racing Green, Top Shop and Hawkshead.

Charles Tyrwhitt

http://www.ctshirts.co.uk

A truly interactive site for buying shirts, since the client can tailor his own shirt by making a choice of pockets, sleeves or collars.

Christian Scott

http://www.christianscott.com

Sweaters and jumpers in cashmere or wool, plus jackets, scarves, throws, rugs, and other accessories. This firm offers what it describes as 'all goods that reflect Scotland'.

Diesel UK Virtual Store

http://ukstore.diesel.com

Men and women will find here their favourite trendy jeans, shirts and jackets. Not forgetting luggage and fragrances.

Freemans

http://www.freemans.com

Galleries of enlargeable thumbnail pictures enable you to choose between everyday fashions to collections from designers, such as Paul Smith, Ben Sherman or Calvin Klein.

Jones Bootmaker

http://www.jonesbootmaker.com

Collection of footwear for men and women: casual, fashion or work shoes. Free delivery provided.

Kays

http://www.kaysnet.com

Kay's online catalogue. More than 25,000 products (fashion, toys, DIY, sports). Free delivery.

Kiniki

http://www.kiniki.com

Top underwear for men: thongs, boxers, briefs and swimwear. There is a gift-finder function.

La Redoute

http://www.redoute.co.uk

More than 800 products are on offer from this French catalogue. The site is in English.

Londonwide

http://www.londonwide.co.uk

Street wear by designers such as Mickey Brazil, Soochi and Nicki Pumkin. A few reductions.

Maple Drive

http://www.mapledrive.com

Quality ladies' lingerie that you can search by brand, size, bra type or brief type. Special offers with up to 60 per cent discount on list prices.

Oswald Bailey

http://www.oswaldbailey.co.uk

Everything you need for outdoor activities: footwear, hiking boots, trousers, jackets, sleeping bags, tents or waterproof clothing.

Outlet Direct

http://www.outletdirect.co.uk

Discount sportswear for men, ladies and kids, with a very large choice of brands (Adidas, British Knights, Diadora, Kickers, Nike, Ralph Lauren, YSL, etc.).

Swerve Clothing UK

http://www.swerve.co.uk

A great range of genuine designer clothes at massive discounts. Top designer labels are represented (Armani, Versace, CK, YSL and others).

Electrical goods for the home

There is an enormous choice on offer in this sector, and you can compare prices, brands and products available. Competition is stiff, so take advantage of this and shop around, without jumping at the first offer that comes along. Don't forget also that some equipment sold abroad will not be compatible with your equipment as technical standards vary from country to country. See 'Technical compatibility' on page 81 for further details.

Electrical Appliances Direct

http://www.electricalappliancesdirect.co.uk

A very big choice of brands in various categories (washing machines, freezers, fans, air-cooling systems, vacuum cleaners, and so on).

Electrical Discount UK

http://www.electricaldiscountuk.co.uk

Plasma TVs, camcorders and DVD players, as well as the whole range of domestic appliances (cookers, microwave ovens, dishwashers, etc.) and very good discounts. Free delivery.

Empiredirect

http://www.empiredirect.co.uk

The top brands in several categories (home entertainment, domestic appliances, hi fi, in-car entertainment). If you find the same item costing less somewhere else during the seven days following your purchase, the company promises you a 120 per cent refund.

Intersaver

http://www.intersaver.co.uk

This online buyers' co-operative offers you bargains grouped into three categories: sound, vision & home office; domestic appliances; and outdoor & garden.

John Lewis

http://www.johnlewis.co.uk

An extensive catalogue in four sectors: refrigeration, laundry, dishwashing and cooking.

Qed-UK

http://www.qed-uk.com

A wide range of products, including TVs, videos and cameras as well as fridges, cookers, and much more, at up to 40 per cent less than the high street price.

Supermarkets, food and drinks

For many of us, having to go to the supermarket is a real chore. Think of the time you can save if you put your order in through the Net and it is delivered to you a few hours later at your chosen location. The convenience, for those for whom mobility is a problem, of not having to leave the home to do the weekly shop is another advantage. The supermarket sector has now joined the online market with a vengeance and has since been taking steps to develop a user-friendly interface for home shopping.

And although the whole of the United Kingdom is not yet covered by all the big supermarket chains, it shouldn't be long before online ordering and doorstep delivery should be possible throughout the United Kingdom.

FifthSense Trading Co.

http://www.fifthsense.com

Flavours from around the world: oils, sauces, marinades, spices, and lots of recipes and nutritional information.

Fresh Food Co.

http://secure.freshfood.co.uk

The UK's largest online organic food store with over 4,000 lines in eight main categories (fresh produce, fish, meat, bakery, groceries & dairy, drinks, ice cream, and specialities). Next-day delivery.

Iceland

http://www.iceland.co.uk

According to its marketing information, Iceland is accessible to 97 per cent of the UK's population. It offers a large range of frozen, chilled and grocery goods, but you have to put in an online order for at least £40 for it to be accepted. You have the possibility of customising your shopping basket for subsequent orders, reflecting your regular choices. A cable TV shopping service should soon be available.

Mad About Wine

http://www.madaboutwine.com

A selection of more than 4,000 wines starting at £3.75 per bottle. If you want some advice, 'Ask the Experts' searches by category or by price.

Sainsbury

http://www.sainsburystoyou.co.uk

A large range of products is on offer from this major UK supermarket chain through its 'To You' online service. Delivery costs £5. For delivery next day, orders must be in by 9.00 p.m. at the latest.

Sunday Times Wine Club

http://www.sundaytimeswineclub.co.uk

Good wines at a range of prices from a well-established mail-order club that is now online too.

Tesco

http://www.tesco.co.uk

Not only grocery articles but also CDs, videos and books are available. 'Bargains of the day' are highlighted to customers. Delivery charge £5.

Waitrose Direct

http://www.waitrose.com

Wine, organic fruit and vegetables, gifts, flowers, books, video and even a travel shop. And the Waitrose@Work scheme invites companies to sign up for an intranet shopping service for businesspeople, where deliveries can be made direct to an office on the same day.

WorldFoods

http://www.worldfoods.co.uk

Organic vegetables and additive-free food are on offer. There is also a nutrition-information section.

Department stores

In the same way that supermarkets have now got the dot-com bug, so too have many of the big department stores. You can browse at your leisure and buy the same goods from your home without having to risk being crushed in the Saturday throng. Payment is also possible by the store's own card, if they have such a scheme.

Argos

http://www.argos.co.uk

One of the major outlets to have done away with expensive front-of-house displays is now on the Net, though you have to wave goodbye to the little pens and forms.

Debenhams

http://www.debenhams.co.uk

The ubiquitous high-street store that has a good range of clothing, gifts, cookware, toys, electrical items and more for the home.

JC Penney

http://www.jcpenney.com

A monster US store that has almost everything.

Fortnum & Mason

http://www.fortnumandmason.co.uk

The posh person's London store that sells everything, at price of course. Sadly, being the virtual version, you cannot experience the plush carpets, or sweep grandly past the doormen of the 'real store'.

Macys

http://www.macys.com

The famous New York store that featured in the 1947 film *Miracle on 34th Street*, is billed as the world's largest store and occupies a whole block.

Marks and Spencer

http://www.marks-and-spencer.co.uk

The popular high-street store with a reputation for quality and a wonderful returns policy.

Wal-Mart

http://www.wal-mart.com

Another US giant that now owns Asda. Prices are low and the store covers a very wide range of categories.

Music

Together with books, the music CD business is another important sector of online shopping. There are many outlets to be found in both domains. Of course, you'll find the giants of the sector offering vast catalogues and chart albums at competitive prices. But there are also independent record retailers who, though their range is smaller, make it possible to find treasures outside the mainstream.

There is also nowadays a trend towards controlled (i.e. payable) distribution of music in MP3 format to counter the piracy that, for many, has become something of a sport. There is a complicated legal debate surrounding the questions of copyright and privacy raging today; but, provided that you are downloading and copying MP3 files for personal use only, from a legitimate MP3 site, you will be ok. Some tracks are free, but you have to pay for others. However, it is not legal to make your own CDs to distribute or sell.

If you are looking for the best-selling albums at the best price, start with the bargain-finders, such as ShopSmart (http://www.shopsmart.co.uk) or myTaxi (http://www.mytaxi.co.uk).

101cd.com

http://www.101cd.com

This site has a catalogue of more than one-and-a-half million CDs, videos, DVDs, books and computer games.

Amazon

http://www.amazon.co.uk

It's difficult to talk about books or CDs without mentioning Amazon. An enormous choice is available, as you would expect, and the site has easy searching (by category, title, musicians, etc.).

Audiostreet

http://www.audiostreet.infront.co.uk

A stock of more than 50,000 CDs and numerous samples are on offer in 'real audio'. Free delivery.

BOL

http://www.uk.bol.com

Books Online also supplies music. It has a catalogue of 500,000 titles, plus news, interviews, recommendations and music chronicles. Free delivery.

Borrow Or Rob

http://www.borroworrob.com

Around 750,000 CDs can be supplied, and many of them are at half the list price. Free delivery world-wide.

CD Paradise

http://www.cdparadise.com

This online music store from W.H. Smith offers more than 200,000 titles and reductions of up to 25 per cent on list price. And CD Paradise also offers a 'Do Your Own

CDs' service where customers can select their choice of tracks from those available on the site.

CD-WOW!

http://www.cd-wow.co.uk

A large number of new releases for just £8.99. And delivery is free, even at that price.

Magpie records

http://www.magpierecords.co.uk

The latest dance, indie, rock and reggae releases.

MDC ClassicMusic

http://www.mdcmusic.co.uk

An independent record retailer who loves classical music, not just what the supermarkets have to sell.

DVD and video

Many sites have launched sales of video tapes and DVDs, so there's no lack of choice. The problem is more one of finding new films to your liking. Many sales outlets make suggestions or offer you the latest issues. But you can also consult a databank on cinema and make a search by actor, director, film type, etc. A good address for doing this is The Internet Movie Database (http://www.imdb.com).

Don't be tempted by US sites, because their video and DVD systems are not compatible with Europe's (see 'Technical compatibility' page 81). Standards vary even within Europe; for example, a colour video manufactured for French video players will only play in black and white on a UK machine.

Amazon

http://www.amazon.co.uk

As with books and music, Amazon is a leader in the DVD/video field, too. As usual, an impressive choice is available; and there are facilities for searching by title, actor or director.

Bensons World of Home Entertainment

http://www.bensonsworld.co.uk

An abundant catalogue showing the latest video titles to come out and a selection of DVDs at £9.99. Free postage on all UK video orders.

Blackstar

http://www.blackstar.co.uk

A large catalogue, with easy searching and free delivery.

DVDream

http://www.dvdream.co.uk

A good selection at interesting prices. The DVDs on offer are only for Zone 2 (see page 81).

DVDstreet

http://www.dvdstreet.infront.co.uk

All the latest films and some considerable price reductions. Quoted prices include VAT and UK delivery charges.

FilmWorld

http://www.filmworld.co.uk

A website address to keep in mind for cinema enthusiasts. Many rare films, original cuts, interviews and news on less mainstream or arthouse cinema.

Travel

The Web doesn't just take you on virtual travels; it also gives you the means to plan a trip to any destination in the real world. You no longer need to traipse from one travel agency to another. The Web enables you to hunt down the best deals in the comfort of your own home. Just compare the prices (or a shopbot can do this for you), you make your choice, and then you place your reservations. You can do this three months in advance or on the day before you leave if there is availability. The last-minute deals on offer can be real bargains, if you are willing to be flexible about destination.

Many sites offer you supplementary information (or Web links to it) enabling you to find out more about the location you're going to visit. Take a look at sites such as Lonely Planet (**http://www.lonelyplanet.com**), Rough Guides (**http://www.roughguides.com**) or the Columbus World Travel Guide (**http://www.travel-guides.com**), which give you further background information on places around the world.

Before paying for an Internet booking, always check the conditions and details of the trip carefully. Do this even if it means sending an e-mail to get further clarification. In this way you will avoid potential unpleasant surprises when you reach your destination.

A2bTravel

http://www.a2btravel.com

Trains, planes, buses, ferries, car-hire, UK mapping, accommodation of all kinds – everything you need for travelling in the United Kingdom.

Bargainholidays.com

http://www.bargainholidays.com

A very wide selection of flights and package holidays, with last-minute offers and a search module for cut-price flights at £99 or £199.

Cheapflights.com

http://www.cheapflights.co.uk

This is not a travel agency but the place to find the best deals to any destination. So it is more of a portal and search engine than anything else. An e-mail alert service can keep you up to date on special deals coming through.

EBookers

http://www.ebookers.com

An excellent address for reserving flights, hotels, car hire and holidays and for consulting supersaves of the day. They offer a fare-alert service.

Eurostar

http://www.eurostar.com

Timetables, prices and reservations online for the Eurostar to France or Belgium.

Expedia

http://www.expedia.msn.co.uk

A very comprehensive site by Microsoft: flights, hotels, cars, holidays and business travel. There are also 'Best Deals', or the 'Fare Tracker' service to get weekly fare updates by e-mail.

HotelWorld

http://www.hotelworld.com

Thousands of hotels throughout the world are advertised here. Search by city, name, or on the atlas. HotelWorld offers a large number of reductions, sometimes even in luxury hotels. You can also find special deals for quality apartments.

Lastminute.com

http://www.lastminute.com

Last-minute deals for flights, hotels and holidays (as well as sections on entertainment and auctions). And a newsletter service so you don't miss out on anything. You don't need to wait till the last minute to find bargains.

Snow-forecast

http://www.snow-forecast.com

Has global warming hit the pistes too? Check out the latest cold fronts in over 30 different countries. Updated twice daily.

The Train Line

http://www.thetrainline.com

For reserving mainline train tickets in the United Kingdom. Search timetables and prices.

Travelocity

http://www.travelocity.co.uk

All the resources you can dream of to organise your trip: flights, cars, hotels, city breaks, weekend deals, currency converter, destination guides and the best-fare finder.

Airline sites

Aer Lingus

http://www.aerlingus.ie

Aeroflot

http://www.aeroflot.org

Air Canada

http://www.aircanada.ca

Alitalia

http://www.italiatour.com

American

http://www.americanair.com

British Airways

http://www.british-airways.com

British Midland

http://www.iflybritishmidland.com

Delta

http://www.delta.com

EasyJet

http://www.easyjet.co.uk

Go

http://www.go-fly.com

KLM

http://www.klmuk.com

Ryanair

http://www.ryanair.com

SAS

http://www.sas.se

TWA

http://www.twa.com

United

http://www.ual.co.uk

Virgin

http://www.virgin-atlantic.com

Flowers and gifts

With the Web, you no longer have no excuse for forgetting someone's birthday. Many sites are happy to remind you by e-mail of a date set by you in advance. And if you've run out of ideas, they will be there to give you suggestions of all kinds. Nor is the issue of time available for choosing a gift for someone any longer so significant, because sending a bouquet of flowers through an online florist (or arranging any other similar gift) will take you just a few minutes.

Clare Florist

http://www.clareflorist.co.uk

Hand-tied bouquets, baskets and flower arrangements. Free delivery for the next day.

Flowers Direct

http://www.flowersdirect.co.uk

From the most luxuriant to the simplest, all styles of bouquets and suggestions for special occasions. A reminder service for the forgetful.

Interflora

http://www.interflora.co.uk

A very large selection of flowers. You can design your own bouquet or follow Interflora's suggestions. Delivery abroad is also possible.

Gifts

Best of British

http://www.thebestofbritish.com

A large choice of designer gifts: hampers, handbags, and fashion items for men and women.

Firebox

http://www.firebox.com

An eclectic choice of surprising objects for all purses and all tastes. Free delivery.

Go Bazaar

http://www.gobazaar.co.uk

From the practical to the eccentric, gadgets of all kinds and free delivery.

Hamper.com

http://www.hamper.com

'A store dedicated to all things delicious': chocolates, wines, port and stilton cheese, smoked salmon, and so on.

Hugs and Cuddles

http://www.hugsandcuddles.co.uk

Teddy bears and other soft toys can be delivered throughout the world.

Kitsch & Retro Online

http://www.kitsch.co.uk

The empire of kitsch in all its splendour. Lava Lamps, Chilli Lights, Japanese Robots, Barbie Dolls – and more. 'The weirdest and most wonderful.'

Online Jewellery Shop

http://www.onlinejewelleryshop.com

A wide selection of rings, necklaces, bracelets and cuff-links and a 14-day money-back guarantee.

Oxfam Fair Trading Online

http://oxfam.org.uk/shop/

Craft objects from the Philippines, El Salvador, Indonesia and most of Africa, including musical instruments. You get some good gift ideas and you support the people behind the products in the developing world to get a fair deal.

Worthaglance

http://www.worthaglance.com

Considerable reductions in five categories, one of which is gift ideas (the others being household, electrical, toys and leisure).

Greetings cards

All Yours

http://www.all-yours.net/postcard

A virtual card site – perfect if you have only remembered the occasion on the day and so don't have time to post a card. Choose a design, enter the destination e-mail address, your-mail address, a message, and then click **Deliver**. Your virtual card wil be sent completely free of charge, except for the time spent on the Net.

American Greetings

http://www.americangreetings.com

Both virtual and 'real' cards to choose from.

Cyber Card

http://www.cybercard.co.uk

You can choose and personalise a 'real' greetings card with your own text and even your own photos.

Hallmark Cards

http://www.hallmark.com

The high-street store is now online – and offering both virtual and 'real' cards – and you can also order flowers and chocolates.

Computing

Most retailers and manufacturers of computer equipment have not been slow to promote online sales, and these constitute an increasing part of their turnover. This is therefore a highly competitive sector that enables you to make considerable savings.

Will a basic 'family' package be enough for you, or are you looking for a top-of-the-range desktop? Whether or not you are clear about your requirements, it might be useful to have a look at a specialist site that analyses the different products on the market, such as ZDNet (**http://www.zdnet.co.uk**).

Many sites enable you to configure and price the model you are considering, and guide you through the process. It's not just for the experts, and will enable you to have a machine made to measure, in accordance with your needs and financial resources. Don't forget to check whether the price displayed includes VAT and delivery charges.

In relation to software, most hardware systems come with pre-packaged software, and many other software products can be purchased from online (or high-street) computer stores to add on to a system. In addition, it is possible to download software from Internet sites, either for a fee (through another online financial transaction) or as **shareware** or **freeware**.

The advantage for the manufacturer of selling software in this way is that when an order is received the software can simply be copied and despatched via the Internet; there is no need to hold stock. For the buyer, there is no expensive packaging to pay for, so the buyer immediately benefits from this too.

To download software, after you have clicked on the link offering the software, there will be a box asking for confirmation that you wish to download. You then have two choices: saving the file onto a diskette (the safest method) or running it directly onto your hard disk. If you run directly you have to choose where to keep the file, usually in your Downloaded Documents folder.

Having chosen where to keep the file, click on **Save** and the file will start downloading. To use the software, you now have to install it. Locate the file, double-click on it and installation will proceed.

Manufacturers

Apple

http://www.apple.com/ukstore

Damson Computers

http://www.sbs-sales.co.uk/damson

Dan

http://www.dan.co.uk

Dell

http://www.dell.co.uk

Elonex

http://www.elonex.co.uk

Evesham Micros

http://www.evesham.co.uk

Gateway

http://www.gw2k.co.uk

Hewlett Packard

http://www.hewlett-packard.com/uk

Tiny

http://www.uk.tiny.com

Viglen

http://www.viglen.co.uk

Online stores

Action

http://www.action.com

A well-stocked catalogue of software and hardware, accessories and components, as well as product reviews, benchmark tests and opinions by Ziff-Davis. Delivery charges vary, depending on location and weight.

Buy.com

http://www.gb.buy.com

Computers, software, consumables, digital imaging – the choice is considerable, and some of the offers are really eye-catching.

Computer Warehouse Online

http://www.cwonline.co.uk

A site with all Mac products. You can receive a newsletter, and delivery is free for every purchase over £30.

Dabs

http://www.dabs.com

Toshiba, HP, Compaq, Epson, Mac, Creative Labs are all here, as well as many others. They also have webcams and DVD players. Free delivery.

Insight

http://www.insight.com/uk

A large choice of software and hardware from the major brands. Weekly deals, best-sellers, lots of information on products, and competitive prices.

Jungle.com

http://www.jungle.com

A very wide range of hardware, software, peripherals, consumables and downloads. Easy searching and competitive prices.

Micro Warehouse UK Ltd.

http://www.microwarehouse.co.uk

Notebooks, desktops, PDA organisers, Mac items, new products, best deals and the possibility of comparing prices within a particular category. Free delivery.

Simply Computers

http://www.simply.co.uk

A good address for configuring a computer to suit you.

Software and games

Chips World

http://www.chipsworld.co.uk

A large choice of quality games at very reasonable prices.

Games Paradise

http://www.gamesparadise.com

A 'paradise' in which W.H. Smith offers games for the Sony PlayStation, Nintendo 64 and PC. Everything is accompanied by charts, reviews and special offers.

LearningStore

http://www.educational.co.uk

More than 1,000 educational programs for children, covering various domains: music, languages, history, geography, science and nature, computing, and so on.

PC cards direct

http://www.pccardsdirect.co.uk

A wide range of laptop and PDA add-ons and cards for digital cameras.

Simplygames

http://www.simplygames.co.uk

A good website for buying the latest arrivals in the world of games (for PC, PlayStation, Nintendo 64, and Dreamcast) without going bankrupt.

Software First

http://www.softwarefirst.com

All the games you can think of for Mac, PC, PlayStation, Nintendo 64, etc. – the home page lists chart-toppers in each category. And there are also free downloads and an auctions section.

Software Paradise

http://www.softwareparadise.co.uk

This portal enables you to find your way round the 100,000 available titles (for Mac, PC and Linux), including the latest arrivals. Free delivery.

Games and toys

If you want to avoid spending your Saturday in toy shops, why not choose one on the Web? You can then do your choosing in peace and quiet, without having to deal with the incessant pleading of your youngsters as you traipse past miles of display shelves.

Dawson & Son

http://www.dawson-and-son.co.uk

A traditional selection of wooden toys and games for all ages: imaginative games, creative games, educational games, jigsaws, etc.

eToys

http://www.etoys.co.uk

It would be difficult not to find something here that children (of all ages) would dream of having. Searching is possible by age range, type of toy, or brand.

Game Shop Online

http://www.gameshops.co.uk

A large choice of quality board games: backgammon, solitaire, mah-jong, chess and younger children's games.

In2Toys

http://in2toys.com

Toys in quantity and for all ages. And big reductions on quite a lot of them.

Mail Order Express

http://www.moetoys.co.uk

Pre-school toys, modular constructions, bags, children's furniture, wooden toys, puzzles and less traditional games.

Toys 'Я' Us

http://www.toysrus.co.uk

You select the toys by brand, product category, theme/character, age or price. A very good selection is on offer that will be tempting not just to children.

Toyworld Store

http://www.toyworldstore.com

All the traditional games classified by categories.

Toy zone

http://www.toyzone.co.uk

'Where toys hang out' as the site proclaims. Everything from the latest 'must have' fad to puzzles, teddy bears, and educational and outdoor toys. Batteries and gift wrapping are on offer too.

Home and gardening

Decorating, furnishing, DIY work or gardening are occupying a growing space on the Web, as they are in real life. The time given over to leisure, as well as the cost of labour, are factors in this phenomenon. What's more, many sites also offer comprehensive advice on choice of décor, materials or how to do your DIY.

Argos

http://www.argos.co.uk

The online version of this chain of stores, with a considerable number of items classified by category: baby and nursery, DIY and gardening, domestic appliances, furniture, sports and leisure, toys, etc.

Birstall Garden Centre

http://www.birstall.co.uk

You'll find all you need for gardening here: seeds, plants, tools, greenhouses, as well as tips of the day.

British Gardening Online

http://www.oxalis.co.uk

Links to dozens of gardening specialists and lots of articles and tips.

The Cooks Kitchen

http://www.kitchenware.co.uk

A wide range of kitchen products: kettles, teapots, knives, pans, and so on.

Cookson's Tools

http://www.cooksons.com

Over 50,000 tools, both hand- and power-driven. All prices are exclusive of VAT.

DIYTools.com

http://www.diytools.com

All kinds of power tools and hand tools from top manu-facturers. And a forum for handy tips.

E-Vivo

http://www.e-vivo.com

Accessories and furniture of all kinds for the home and office, set out into 12 'departments' like a real store.

Linenstore

http://www.homelinens.co.uk

Curtaining and upholstery fabrics, duvets, pillows, blankets, towels, bathrobes and all kinds of household textiles.

McCord Online

http://www.mccord.uk.com

The online version of the McCord catalogue, with furnishing and accessories for the living room, kitchen, bedroom, bathroom and garden. The website also has a section on 'gifts & ideas' and 'kids stuff'.

10

Frequently asked questions about shopping online

Set out below are some questions about online shopping that are frequently asked, and answers that aim to give insight into this aspect of using the Web. The same topics are covered earlier in this book, and in a little more depth there, where appropriate.

1. Can I do my shopping on the Web in security?

In most cases there's no problem, provided that you follow elementary rules of security (just as in a real shop). Most shopping sites emphasise their policy on secure transactions with the aid of a secure server, and it is worth reading that policy to establish the conditions applicable to making a transaction. But if no information is offered on this subject, don't trust the organisation.

In all cases, keep track of your order by printing it out or saving it on your hard disk. Never send credit card details by e-mail.

2. How can I establish whether a site is secure or not?

You should see a note on the organisation's home page or a link to a security policy assuring you that transactions are effected through a secure server. If in doubt, you should be able to check this point in the website's Help section.

When you have to enter your credit/debit card details, your browser should display a message telling you that you are entering a secure zone. In addition, a closed padlock should appear at the bottom of your screen.

3. Do Cookies threaten my security?

Not at all. Big sites send cookies (special mini-files) to your hard disk to keep track of your visits and to recognise you when you visit them subsequently.

4. Can a hacker get hold of my credit card number?

If you send your bank details through a secure server, there's almost no chance that a hacker will get hold of your secret details. Take assurance from the fact that MasterCard and Visa encourage transactions on the Net to the point of covering you against fraud, and that Amazon, amongst others, will reimburse you for the minimum liability required by the banks.

5. How is it reasonable to make a purchase without first having seen the merchandise?

This question has already been asked with regard to the more traditional mail-order catalogues. However, on the Net, the user also has a lot of information at his or her disposal about the products on sale: specialist sites, shopbots, advice and tips from other consumers, assessments by journalists, etc. In addition, communications by e-mail make it possible to establish relations easily and quickly between sellers and buyers.

6. Can I go shopping on a foreign site?

The Net has no frontiers, and so take advantage of it. But find out whether the site you're visiting makes deliveries to your physical location and what the company charges for them, not forgetting customs duties and VAT.

Don't forget as well to check for technical compatibility, particularly for electrical and electronic equipment coming from the United States. In the same way, check that DVDs are compatible with your own zone.

Finally, make sure you know your rights with regard to any product guarantee offered. Is it also valid in your own country?

7. Does everything cost less on the Net?

If you have a business on the Web, this is clearly the message you want to get across. Even though the Web certainly enables traders to reduce many costs, offline trading still has a bright future. It's always advisable to find out the prices in your local high-street before doing your searches on the Net. And make sure you're not paying any hidden costs that take you unawares.

8. Can I do my shopping at any online business?

In principle, yes. But some of them don't sell to countries abroad. This is the case with many US traders.

Even for UK traders, you need to make sure that they will deliver to your own region. Some supermarkets, for instance, don't cover the whole country (yet) for deliveries.

9. What about VAT and excise duty for foreign goods?

There is no VAT for goods worth less than £18 (including delivery charges) or for certain goods such as books or food.

Within the European Union you only have to pay excise duty on alcohol and tobacco.

Purchases made outside the European Union are liable to any or all of these charges: customs duty, VAT and excise duty. For more details, see Chapter 6 entitled 'Buying from abroad'.

Glossary
and
Index

Glossary

Set out below are definitions of words related to online shopping, some of which occur in the preceding text and are highlighted in ***bold italics*** at first occurrence. In addition, there are technical terms that some readers might not be familiar with, and that are thus defined here as an aid.

Authentication

The procedure used in the electronic transactions to ensure the security of correspondence. It consists of checking the identity of the parties (through password, electronic signature, etc.).

Back office

Everything concerning the operations generated by an (online or offline) transaction: taking an order, payment, electronic receipt, delivery, etc.

Buy-cycle

A group buying offer, open for a certain period. The buying price of the goods on offer depends on the number of buyers brought together before the close of the buying session.

Buying guide

Advice and information offered to help a consumer make online purchases.

Cart

The virtual shopping-basket in which a consumer collects all purchases before dealing with payment.

Certificate Authority (CA)

A third party that verifies the identity and reliability of a trading site and that confers on it a certificate, which will be displayed on the site.

'Clicks and mortar'

A term used to describe firms from the 'old' economy that are developing strategies for the Web. The term is in contrast to the more familiar 'bricks and mortar', which designates firms absent from the Web.

Cookie

A small file that certain websites upload on to your hard disk when you visit them, so that they can find your 'profile' when you visit them again and thereby personalise some of their marketing. See also *Profile*, below.

Digital certificate

A certificate proving the existence of a physical address for an online business. This provides increased reliability.

Directory

A directory of websites classified by categories and subcategories. Yahoo! is a famous general example, but there are other shopping directories listed in this book.

Distance selling

The process by which a sale or transaction takes place without a meeting between the seller and the buyer. This is the case with sales by mail order, from a catalogue or over the Net.

Domain name

In an Internet address, the portion that designates the host of the site. For example, the domain name of **http://www.bbc.co.uk** will be bbc.co.uk.

E-mail alert

A service that lets a potential customer know by e-mail about the latest deals that relate to the customer's profile or specifically indicated preferences that shouldn't be missed. All a customer has to do is enter an appropriate specification and e-mail address at the relevant website.

Electronic wallet

The payment system enabling its holder to credit an account for paying for online purchases.

Encryption

The procedure whereby, when an online transaction is being made, it is possible to hide the information exchanged between seller and buyer from third parties. Confidential information, such as a bank card number, can only be decoded with a specific key. This procedure is essential to ensure the security of transactions on the Web.

Escrow

The process of using an intermediary in a commercial transaction. The intermediary holds the amount paid by the buyer and sends it to the sender when the goods have been delivered according to the terms agreed upon.

Flag

An interactive advertising banner that makes it possible to access an advertiser's site with a click of the mouse.

Freeware

Software that you can download from a website free of charge.

Front office

In relation to websites, everything involved in the procedures of creating a trading site and managing its catalogue.

Goodwill policy

Some commercial sites offer consumers some benefits or protection that they are not legally obliged to offer. This is called goodwill policy.

Hacker

A term used to describe those who break into databases, either for fun or for less noble motives.

Help section

You will often find a Help link on a website's home page. This represents a sort of user manual for the site, and when you need to find an answer to a question regarding the site, you may find the answer there.

Home page

A website's reception page – the first one to appear when you access the site from its standard web address.

Hot site

Any site that is popular and attracts a large number of visitors, either because it is fashionable or because of exceptional content.

HTML (Hypertext Markup Language)

The language used to create documents and website pages on the World Wide Web.

Micro-payment

A description of a payment of less than £5.00, which is not acceptable by bank card so that another form of payment has to be used (an electronic wallet, for example).

Order confirmation

A message sent by a trader to a customer to let the customer know that an online order placed by the customer has been recorded and is being followed up.

Portal

A site that offers a large range of services and content, such as e-mail, chat, directory, search engine, weather, channels,…

Privacy policy

Policy of a website under which the site undertakes to keep secret any information it has gathered on customers and not to pass this information on to others – to prevent customers being inundated with e-mail (spam).

Profile

Information on the interests and preferences of a consumer. The profile thus created by a Web trader will make it possible to send the customer targeted advertising messages.

Real audio

Standard developed by the RealNetworks company for contiuous transmission (streaming) of audio or video files over the Net.

Repudiation

Legal right granted to a buyer to contest a distance-selling transaction effected without consent and yet with the buyer's bank card. This right may be exercised for 90 working days after the bank account has been debited and obliges the seller to reimburse in full the amount he has collected.

Search engine

A tool allowing the automatic searching, using one or more keywords, of millions of Web pages to find sites corresponding to these words.

Secure server

A server covering one or more traders that is able to protect confidential information with the aid of various encryption techniques.

Secured payment

Any payment benefiting from a security system for data being exchanged (such as SET and SSL).

SET (Secure Electronic Transaction)

A transaction security standard developed by Visa and MasterCard, Netscape, IBM and others. It provides a high degree of security for online payments by credit card.

Shareware

Software that you can download and that is normally free of charge for a limited period of time.

Shopbot

A search engine making it possible to compare the prices quoted on the Web for a particular product. The word is a contraction of 'shopping' and 'robot'.

Shopping directory

See *Directory*, above.

Shopping mall

Virtual equivalent of a commercial centre where, on the same site, a large number of vendors can be found.

S-HTTP (Secure Hypertext Transfer Protocol)

Encryption standard supported by AOL and CompuServe online services. It is denoted in web addresses with the letters 'https' (rather than just 'http') at the front of the address.

SSL (Secure Socket Layer)

A protocol widely adopted on trading websites that makes it possible to hide customers' confidential information such as bank card details.

Tracking system

A system, set up by a supplier, making it possible for a customer as well as the supplier to follow the course of an order to its final destination.

URL (Uniform Resource Locator)

The address of a site on the Web.

Index